Artichoke Recipes

Finding the Heart of the Story in Journey of Life

With "Auntie Artichoke"

History of the Artichoke 3
Legend of the Artichoke 6
How to Select and Store an Artichoke 7
Nutrition Facts About Artichokes 8
How to Prepare and Cook an Artichoke 9
How to Eat an Artichoke 11
How to Clean Artichoke Hearts 12
Artichoke Recipes 13
    Baked Artichoke 14
    Artichoke and Spinach Dip 16
    Three Cheese Hot Artichoke Dip 18
    Stuffed Artichokes 19
    Hot Artichoke Crab Dip 21
    Artichoke Hummus 23
    Cream of Artichoke Soup 25
    Potato-Artichoke Soup 27
    Cheesy Artichoke Stuffed Shells 29
    Chicken Tagine with Artichoke Hearts and Peas 31
    Sautéed Baby Artichokes with Roast Chicken Parts 33
    Artichoke Cheesecake 35
    Grilled Baby Artichokes with Blood Oranges and Thyme .. 37
    Warm Artichokes with Harissa-White Bean Dip 39
    Artichoke and Black Olive Tapenade in Radicchio Cups 41
ARTI-JOKES 43
Who is Judy H. Wright aka Auntie Artichoke & What's with the Artichoke? 45
Resources for Parents, Teachers and other Caring Adults 47

Letter from Auntie Artichoke

Hello from beautiful Montana,

As a global speaker and writer on family issues, I am frequently asked why I would have chosen an artichoke as my logo. You will find the answers in other essays included in this little book, but I do want to share my enthusiasm for finding the heart of the story in the journey of life.

Part of my community volunteerism is hearing and recording end-of-life stories for Hospice. According to a study done and my own experience, the three things most dying people regret are:

They wish they would have risked more. My mother said she chose the known and the unknown would have been fine.

They wish they would have reflected more. Just stopped along the way to think "Is this the kind of person I want to be?"

They wish they would have contributed more. One man told me that he wished he would have shared his wisdom with his sons. Another said she wished they would have had more people over for dinner and not worried about the stained carpet.

As I learned these lessons, I removed some outer leaves of doubt and fear. When I dared to open my heart and really accept the pointy edges and the fuzzy parts, my life changed. So much better in fact, I am amazed and grateful for the blessings and opportunities that have come to our lives.

It is my deepest with that you find that same peace and joy in your heart.

Hopefully, we will meet in person one day and share a cup of tea and exchange stories. Until then, please know that you are loved and appreciated.

Fondly,

Judy Helm Wright aka "Auntie Artichoke"

History of the Artichoke

Artichokes are a delicious treat with an interesting history. They are a perennial in the thistle family and are believed to be native to the Mediterranean and Canary Islands. The name comes from the Italian words Aticiocco and articoclos.

There are more than 140 varieties of artichoke, but only 40 of those are produced for commercial use.

These are produced in France, Italy and Spain, but in the US all artichokes are produced in California.

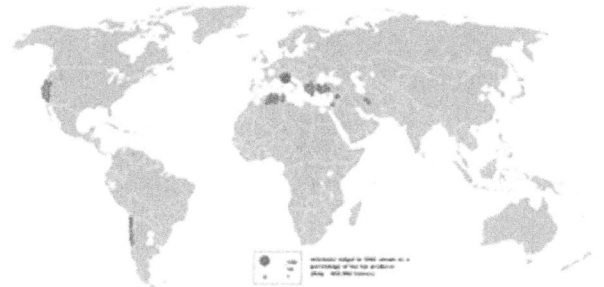

Fully grown, they can cover an area about six feet in diameter and be three to four feet high. The part that we eat is actually the flower bud.

These buds can grow as large as seven inches in diameter and are a violet color. Though they flower all year round their peak seasons are spring and fall.

Artichokes have been written about since the time of Christ. The Greeks and Romans considered artichokes a delicacy as well as an aphrodisiac. The Romans believed that consuming artichokes would ensure their women would give birth to boys. In 800 AD, the North African Moors began cultivating artichokes in Granada and Spain, while the Saracens began cultivating them in Sicily. Between 800 AD and 1500 AD, the techniques for cultivating artichokes were perfected and they were often grown in monastery gardens.

After the fall of the Roman Empire the artichoke all but disappeared, until the Renaissance when they re-emerged.  Catharine de Medici was credited with making the artichoke famous when she brought them from Italy to France when she married King Henry II in the mid-16th century. French immigrants brought the artichoke to the New World in the early 1800s when they settled in the Louisiana Territory

The first commercial artichokes were produced in Louisiana, but by 1940 they had completely disappeared from the area.

Spaniards brought the artichoke to California's Monterey area during the late 1800s. A landowner in the Salinas Valley of Monterey County, California, just south of San Francisco, decided to lease his land previously dedicated to the growing of sugar beets to Italian farmers that he encouraged to try growing the "new" vegetable. His reasons were economic as artichokes were fetching high prices and farmers could pay him triple what the sugar company did for the same land.

In the early 20th century the California artichokes were selling for 30 to 40 cents each in Boston. In the 20th century the Mafia in the North Eastern US controlled the artichoke trade.

Legend of the Artichoke

According to an Aegean legend, the first artichoke was a lovely young girl who lived on the island of Zinari.

The god Zeus was visiting his brother Poseidon. As Zeus emerged from the sea, he saw a beautiful young mortal woman. He was so pleased with the girl, whose name was Cynara, he decided to make her a goddess. Zeus anticipated that when his wife Hera was away, there would be many trysts between himself and Cynara. However, Cynara soon missed her mother and grew homesick.

After she snuck back to the mortal world, Zeus was so enraged with her un-goddess-like behavior that he hurled Cynara back to earth and transformed her into the plant we now know as the artichoke.

The artichoke takes a bit of work for the eater, just as Cynara represented more work than Zeus wished to spend on her.

How to Select and Store an Artichoke

Artichokes should be deep green dense leaves, they should be firm and weighty (as they lose water they lose weight).

You should buy them with the intention of using them right away. Fresh is best, but you can store them for one to two days in the refrigerator.

If you can't use them immediately you should cut them off about ½ inch away from the stem, wrap in damp paper towels and store in a plastic bag.

Nutrition Facts About Artichokes

Artichokes are free of fat, saturated fat and cholesterol. (unless you cook them in oil)

Also, artichokes are low in sodium and in calories (just 25 calories for 1 artichoke, none from fat) –

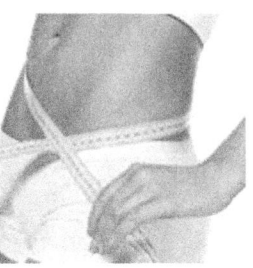

Not only are they non-fattening, they are also an excellent source of plant-based protein (about 4 grams in one medium artichoke)

Artichokes are a good source of fiber, vitamin C, folate and magnesium. They also contain cynarin which gives them their sweet taste

This information compliments of Simply Recipes http://simplyrecipes.com/recipes/how_to_cook_and_eat_an_artichoke/

How to Prepare and Cook an Artichoke

1. If the artichokes have little thorns on the end of the leaves, take a kitchen scissors and cut of the thorned tips of all of the leaves. This step is mostly for aesthetics as the thorns soften with cooking and pose no threat to the person eating the artichoke.

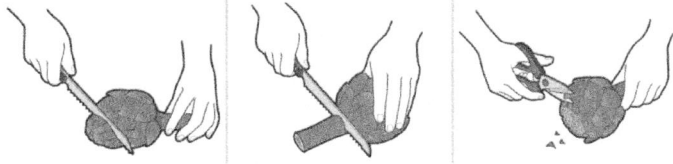

2. Slice about 3/4 inch to an inch off the tip of the artichoke.

3. Pull off any smaller leaves towards the base and on the stem.

4. Cut excess stem, leaving up to an inch on the artichoke. The stems tend to be more bitter than the rest of the artichoke, but some people like to eat them.

Alternatively you can cut off the stems and peel the outside layers which is more fibrous and bitter and cook the stems along with the artichokes.

5. Rinse the artichokes in running cold water.

6. In a large pot, put a couple inches of water, a clove of garlic, a slice of lemon, and a bay leaf (this adds wonderful flavor to the artichokes).

Insert a steaming basket. Add the artichokes. Cover. Bring to a boil and reduce heat to simmer.

Cook for 25 to 45 minutes or until the outer leaves can easily be pulled off. Note: artichokes can also be cooked in a pressure cooker (about 15-20 minutes cooking time). Cooking time depends on how large the artichoke is, the larger, the longer it takes to cook.

How to Eat an Artichoke

Artichokes may be eaten cold or hot, but I think they are much better hot. They are served with a dip, either melted butter or mayonnaise. My favorite dip is mayo with a little bit of balsamic vinegar mixed in.

1. Pull off outer petals, one at a time.

2. Dip white fleshy end in melted butter or sauce. Tightly grip the other end of the petal. Place in mouth, dip side down, and pull through teeth to remove soft, pulpy, delicious portion of the petal. Discard remaining petal. Continue until all of the petals are removed.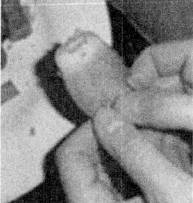

3. With a knife or spoon, scrape out and discard the inedible fuzzy part (called the "choke") covering the artichoke heart. The remaining bottom of the artichoke is the heart. Cut into pieces and dip into sauce to eat.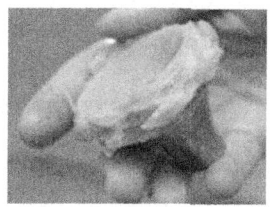

How to Clean Artichoke Hearts

In a large pot with a tight-fitting lid bring about 1 inch water, lemon juice, and 1 tsp. salt to a boil.

Meanwhile, cut stems and thorns from artichokes.

Place artichokes, stem-side down and standing, in pot. Cover, reduce heat to medium-low, and cook until a leaf pulls out easily from each artichoke, about 20 minutes. Drain and rinse with cold water.

Pull off and discard very dark green, outer leaves. Pull off remaining leaves and set aside. Use a spoon to scrape out fuzzy choke.

Cut off any fibrous dark green parts around outside of heart. Roughly chop heart and put in a blender or food processor.

Repeat with remaining artichokes. Use a spoon to scrape off tender flesh from each leaf. Discard leaf and put artichoke flesh in blender with hearts. Repeat with remaining leaves.

Artichoke Recipes

Baked Artichoke

1 whole artichoke
2 garlic cloves, quartered
1/2 lemon, juice from
2 tablespoons olive oil
1/2 teaspoon sea salt
3 tablespoons broth

Directions:

Rinse and trim the artichoke, cutting the stem off straight so that the artichoke can stand up on it's own without tipping over.

Spread artichoke petals open as far as possible without snapping. Between the petals: squeeze lemon juice, drizzle olive oil and broth and stuff garlic. Sprinkle the top of the artichoke with sea salt. Tightly double wrap and seal the artichoke with heavy-duty aluminum foil.

Place artichoke, making sure that it is standing up straight so the liquid doesn't come out (I put them packed together in a baking dish) in a pre-heated 425 oven and bake (medium-sized for 60 minutes, large for 90 minutes). Remove from oven and remove wrapping.

http://www.food.com/recipe/no-fuss-easy-baked-artichoke

Artichoke and Spinach Dip

Original Recipe Yield 10 servings

Ingredients

- 2 - (16 ounce) loaves King's Hawaiian® Sweet Bread
- 1 cup mayonnaise
- 1 cup sour cream
- 1 - (1 ounce) package ranch-style dip mix
- 1 - (14 ounce) can artichoke hearts, drained and chopped
- 1 - (10 ounce) package frozen chopped spinach, thawed and drained
- 1 - (8 ounce) can sliced water chestnuts, drained and chopped
- 1 cup grated Parmesan cheese (optional)

Directions

Preheat oven to 350 degrees F.

Carefully hollow 1 loaf, leaving 1-inch on sides and bottoms. Cube removed bread and additional loaf.

Place bowl and cubes on baking sheets and bake for 10 minutes or until golden brown.

Blend mayo, sour cream and dip; mix together in a large bowl. Add artichoke hearts, spinach and water chestnuts; mix well.

Cover and refrigerate until well chilled. Transfer to bread bowl and serve with toasted bread cubes.

To serve hot: Stir in 1 cup grated Parmesan cheese; microwave on high 4-5 minutes or until hot, stirring occasionally. Transfer dip to bread bowl and serve with toasted bread cubes.

Nutritional Information

Amount Per Serving Calories: 601 | Total Fat: 32.8g | Cholesterol: 74mg

Three Cheese Hot Artichoke Dip

Prep 10 min

Cook 30 min

Total time: 40 min

Yield's 3-4 servings

Ingredients:

- 1 (8 ounces) block cream cheese, softened
- 1 cup mayonnaise
- 1 (14 ounces) can artichoke hearts, drained and chopped
- 2 green onions, sliced thin
- 1/2 cup grated Parmesan
- 1 cup shredded mozzarella
- Dash hot sauce
- Dash Worcestershire sauce
- Salt and pepper

Directions

Preheat oven to 350 degrees F. In a large mixing bowl, beat the cream cheese with a hand held electric mixer until smooth. Then beat in the mayonnaise until smooth. Add remaining ingredients and stir together until combined. Transfer the dip to a pie plate or shallow gratin dish. Bake in a preheated oven for 30 to 40 minutes until the top is golden brown and the dip is bubbling. Serve hot with crackers, tortilla chips, crostini or veggies.

Stuffed Artichokes

Prep 20min

Cook 2 hrs

Total Time 2hr 20min

Yields 4 servings

Ingredients

- 4 cups plain breadcrumbs
- 1 cup grated Parmesan/Romano cheese blend
- 1/2 cup extra-virgin olive oil
- 3 tablespoons chopped fresh flat-leaf parsley
- 5 cloves garlic, minced
- 2 lemons, plus 4 lemon slices
- 1/2 teaspoon salt
- 1/4 teaspoon freshly ground pepper
- 4 large artichokes

Directions

Mix the breadcrumbs, cheese, olive oil, parsley, garlic, the juice from 1 1/2 lemons and the salt and pepper in a large bowl until thoroughly combined.

The mixture should be slightly moist. If it appears very dry, add a small amount of additional lemon juice.

Cut off the stem of each artichoke, and then trim the tips of the leaves with kitchen shears.

Open the leaves with your fingertips and rinse with cold water, holding the leaves open.

Working with one at a time, place each artichoke in the center of the bowl of breadcrumb mixture and stuff the mixture into the leaves, holding the leaves open.

You may have leftover stuffing, depending on the size of the artichokes.

Sprinkle the tops of the artichokes with the juice from the remaining lemon half.

Place a lemon slice on top of each artichoke.

Wrap each artichoke in foil and place in a large pot with 3 cups cold water.

Bring to a boil. Cover and simmer until the leaves are tender, about 2 hours, depending on the size of the artichokes.

You may need to add more water if the water level gets too low.

Hot Artichoke Crab Dip

Prep 10 min

Cook 10 min

Total Time 20 min

Yield 4 to 6 servings

Ingredients

- 1/2 cup crab cake mixture, reserved from Crab Cakes OR see recipe below
- 1 (14-ounce) can artichoke hearts, drained and chopped
- 1 (10-ounce) package frozen chopped spinach, thawed and well drained
- 1 cup lowfat sour cream
- 2 tablespoons chopped fresh parsley leaves
- 1 teaspoon salt-free garlic and herb seasoning
- 1/2 cup grated Parmesan, divided
- 2 pita pockets, cut into wedges
- Assorted vegetables (baby carrots, sliced zucchini, celery stalks)

Directions

Preheat oven to 400 degrees F. In a medium bowl, combine crab cake mixture, artichoke hearts, spinach, sour cream, parsley, seasoning, and 1/4 cup of the Parmesan. Mix well.

Transfer mixture to a shallow baking dish and top with remaining parmesan cheese. Bake 10 to 12 minutes, until dip is hot and cheese is golden. Serve dip with pita wedges and vegetables on the side (or crackers!).

In a large bowl, combine crabmeat, sour cream, oats, bread crumbs, Dijon mustard, crab boil seasoning, oregano, and black pepper. Gently mix ingredients together, being careful not to break up crabmeat.

Yield: about 1 cup

Artichoke Hummus

Prep 10 min

Total Time 10min

Yield 8 servings

Ingredients

- 1 cup canned artichoke hearts, drained
- 1/4 cup fat-free vegetable broth
- 1/4 cup plain fat-free Greek yogurt
- 1 tablespoon lemon juice
- 1 1/2 teaspoons crushed garlic
- 1/2 teaspoon dried parsley flakes, plus more, for optional garnish
- 1/2 teaspoon salt
- 1/4 teaspoon black pepper
- 1/4 teaspoon ground cumin
- 1/4 teaspoon paprika, plus more, for optional garnish
- 1 (15-ounce) can chickpeas (garbanzo beans), drained and rinsed
- Serving suggestion: pita chips, cut veggies

Directions

Put all of the ingredients except for the chickpeas in a blender. Using a potato masher or a fork, thoroughly mash the chickpeas. Transfer to the blender. Puree until smooth, stopping and stirring if blending slows. For best flavor, refrigerate the hummus for several hours. Before serving, garnish with a sprinkle each of paprika and parsley flakes, if you like.

PER SERVING (1/8th of recipe, 1/4 cup): 56 calories, 0.5g fat, 400mg sodium, 9g carbs, 3g fiber, 1g sugars, 3g protein

Cream of Artichoke Soup

This simple puree of artichoke hearts in broth with a bit of garlic and cream is based on one served at Duarte's Tavern in Pescardero, California — not far up the coast from the artichoke growing area around Watsonville and Castroville.

I've lightened the amount of cream a bit (okay, a lot!) to bring out more artichoke flavor. You can make it a bit more elegant by adding a full cup of cream, it is terribly delicious that way, too. Either way you go, it is one of the tastiest soups imaginable.

Note: Avoid the cleaning of the artichokes, or make this out of artichoke season, by using a pound of frozen artichoke hearts, which will most accurately convey the fresh artichoke flavor.

Well drained and rinsed canned artichoke hearts can also be used in a pinch.

Prep Time: 35 minutes

Cook Time: 20 minutes

Total Time: 55 minutes

Ingredients:

- 2 Tbsp. lemon juice or white wine or distilled vinegar
- 1 tsp. salt, plus more to taste
- 6 large artichokes
- 4 cups chicken or vegetables broth
- 1 Tbsp. butter
- 2 cloves garlic, chopped

- 1/2 cup heavy cream or half-and-half
- Freshly ground black or white pepper

Preparation:

In a medium saucepan over medium-high heat melt butter. Add garlic and cook, stirring, until fragrant, about 1 minute.

Transfer garlic to blender with artichokes. Set pan aside.

Whirl artichokes with broth until very smooth. You will need to let the blender run a bit for this to happen-- whirl for at least 2 minutes. This will seem like a long time.

Transfer artichoke mixture to saucepan. Bring to a boil.

Reduce heat to maintain a steady simmer. Add cream, and salt and pepper to taste. Serve hot.

Makes 4 servings.

Potato-Artichoke Soup

8 servings, about 1 cup each

Active Time: 25 minutes

Total Time: 35 minutes

INGREDIENTS

- 1 tablespoon butter
- 1 tablespoon extra-virgin olive oil
- 1 medium onion, chopped
- 1 stalk celery, chopped
- 2 cloves garlic, chopped
- 1 teaspoon chopped fresh thyme or parsley
- 3 cups chopped peeled potatoes (about 1 1/2 pounds)
- 1 9-ounce package frozen artichoke hearts, thawed and chopped
- 4 cups reduced-sodium chicken broth, "no-chicken" broth (see Note) or vegetable broth
- 2 cups water
- 1/2 cup half-and-half (optional)
- 1/2 teaspoon salt
- Freshly ground pepper to taste

PREPARATION

Heat butter and oil in a Dutch oven over medium heat until the butter melts. Add onion and celery; cook, stirring occasionally, until softened, 4 to 6 minutes. Add garlic and thyme (or parsley); cook, stirring, until fragrant, about 10 seconds.

Stir in potatoes and artichoke hearts. Add broth and water; bring to a lively simmer over high heat. Reduce heat to maintain a lively simmer and cook until the vegetables are tender, about 15 minutes.

Puree the soup in the pot using an immersion blender or in batches in a blender. (Use caution when pureeing hot liquids.) Stir in half-and-half (if using), salt and pepper.

TIPS & NOTES

Make Ahead Tip: Cover and refrigerate for up to 4 days or freeze for up to 3 months.

Note: Chicken-flavored broth, a vegetarian broth despite its name, is preferable to vegetable broth n some recipes for its hearty, rich flavor. Sometimes called "no-chicken" broth, it can be found with the soups in the natural-foods section of most supermarkets.

NUTRITION

Per serving: 109 calories; 4 g fat (1 g sat , 2 g mono); 4 mg cholesterol; 17 g carbohydrates; 0 g added sugars; 4 g protein; 3 g fiber; 453 mg sodium; 427 mg potassium.

Cheesy Artichoke Stuffed Shells

Cheesy Artichoke Stuffed Shells is an easy make-ahead pasta main dish recipe perfect for casual entertaining.

Prep Time: 35 minutes

Cook Time: 30 minutes

Total Time: 1 hour, 5 minutes

Ingredients:

- 2 tablespoons butter
- 1 onion, chopped
- 2 cloves garlic, minced
- 1 red bell pepper, chopped
- 1 (8-ounce) package cream cheese, softened
- 1 cup ricotta cheese
- 1/2 cup sour cream
- 1 (14-ounce) can plain artichoke hearts in water, drained and chopped
- 1 cup shredded Monterey Jack cheese
- 1-1/2 cups shredded mozzarella cheese
- 16-ounce box jumbo pasta shells
- 1 (26-ounce) jar pasta sauce
- 1/3 cup grated Parmesan cheese

Preparation:

Preheat oven to 375 degrees F. Bring a large pot of salted water to a boil.

In medium saucepan, melt butter over medium heat. Add onion and garlic; cook and stir for 3 minutes. Add red bell pepper; cook 3-5 minutes longer until vegetables are crisp-tender. Remove from heat.

In large bowl, beat cream cheese until fluffy. Gradually add ricotta cheese and sour cream, beating until combined and smooth. stir in onion mixture and chopped artichoke hearts. Stir in Monterey Jack and mozzarella cheeses.

Cook pasta shells in boiling water until almost tender, according to package directions. Drain well, rinse with cold water, and drain again. Place shells, upside down, on paper towels to drain for 5 minutes.

Stuff shells with cheese mixture. Your fingers are the best tools for this. Place 1 cup pasta sauce in bottom of glass baking dish large enough to hold the shells.

Arrange shells in dish, filled side up. Pour remaining sauce over shells and sprinkle with Parmesan cheese. At this point you can cover the dish and refrigerate for 12-24 hours.

If you're baking immediately, bake for 25-35 minutes until hot and bubbly.

If you're baking the casserole from the refrigerator, add 10-15 minutes to the baking time.

Serves 8

Chicken Tagine with Artichoke Hearts and Peas

Ingredients

- 1 4lb chicken-legs separated into drum and thighs, breast halved crosswise, skin and visible fat removed
- Salt and freshly ground black pepper
- 2 medium onions, --1 coarsely chopped, 1 minced
- 1 1/2 cups of chicken stock or low-sodium chicken broth
- 6 saffron threads, crumbled
- 1/2 teaspoon ground ginger
- 1/2 teaspoon ground coriander
- 1/2 teaspoon ground cumin
- 1/2 teaspoon hot paprika
- 1/4 teaspoon turmeric
- 2 medium tomatoes, cut into eighths
- 1/4 preserved lemon, rind only, minced
- 8 frozen artichoke hearts, thawed and quartered
- 1 cup frozen small peas, thawed

Directions:

Season the chicken pieces with salt and pepper. In a medium, enameled cast-iron casserole, combine the chicken with the coarsely chopped onion and the chicken stock and bring to a boil.

In a small bowl mix the saffron threads with the ginger, coriander, cumin, paprika and turmeric. Stir the spice mixture into the broth.

Cover and simmer over low heat, turning the chicken pieces once, until the breast pieces are just white throughout, about 25 minutes. Transfer the breast pieces to a bowl and cover.

Continue to simmer the drumsticks and thighs covered, until done about 15 minutes longer. Transfer drumsticks and thighs to the bowl with the breast pieces and keep covered.

Add the minced onion, tomatoes, lemon and artichoke hearts to the casserole and simmer gently, turning a few times, until heated through. Serve in shallow bowls.

Sautéed Baby Artichokes with Roast Chicken Parts

Ingredients

- 6 tablespoons extra-virgin olive oil
- 1 3to 4lb chicken trimmed of excess fat and cut into 8 pieces
- Salt and freshly ground black pepper
- 4 small (3 inch long) or 8 baby artichokes
- 1/2 cup chopped fresh parsley leaves
- 2 tablespoons butter
- 8 cloves of garlic, peeled and sliced
- 1/2 cup green olives, pitted and roughly chopped
- Juice of 1/2 lemon plus 4 wedges.

Directions:

Heat the over to 450f. Put 4 tablespoons of olive oil in a roasting pan and put in the oven for a 2-3 minutes to heat the oil.

Add the chicken, turning it a few times to coat it in oil and leave skin side up in roasting pan. Sprinkle with salt and pepper and return the pan to the oven.

While the chicken is roasting clean the artichokes. Cut the top third off each one and remove the outer leaves, stop when you see leaves that are mostly pale green or yellow.

If the stems are tough trim them to within 1/2 inch of the bottom of the artichoke. Cut each artichoke vertically into quarters and use a paring knife to remove the choke.

Note that baby artichokes can just be sliced in half, as they will not have a choke yet.

After the chicken has cooked for 15 minutes, sprinkle on about a third of the parsley and turn the pieces. Sprinkle on another third of the parsley and roast for another 10 minutes.

Turn the chicken over so it is skin side up again, add another third of the parsley and cook until the chicken has clear juice running when you make a small cut into the meat near the bone.

Meanwhile, put the remaining 2 tablespoons of oil and butter into a large skillet over a medium-high heat. When the butter melts ass the artichoke quarters, adjust the heat so they cook steadily without burning.

It will take 10 to 15 minutes for the artichokes to become tender. Add the garlic and olives and continue to cook, stirring occasionally.

The artichokes are done when lightly browned and a little crisp yet tender throughout. Serve the chicken surrounded by the artichoke mixture. Sprinkle all with lemon juice and more parsley. Serve with additional lemon wedges.

Artichoke Cheesecake

Ingredients

- 2 6oz jars of marinated artichokes, drained
- 8 green onions with greens, chopped
- 16 oz ricotta cheese
- 1 cup grated parmesan cheese
- 1 cup shredded Monterey Jack cheese
- 1/2 cup sour cream
- 4 eggs, lightly beaten
- 2 tablespoons of all-purpose flour
- 1/2 teaspoon dry leaf tarragon, crumbled
- 1/2 teaspoon dry leaf oregano, crumbled
- 1/4 teaspoon dry leaf thyme, crumbled
- 1/8 teaspoon dry leaf sage, crumbled
- 1/4 teaspoon pepper
- 6 sheets filo or phyllo dough
- 1/4 cup melted butter

Directions:

Coarsely chop the artichokes; combine in a bowl with chopped green onion, ricotta, Parmesan, and Monterey Jack cheeses, sour cream, eggs, flour, tarragon, oregano, thyme, and pepper. Blend well. Brush butter on a layer of filo dough and place in a 9-inch springform pan, letting it drape up and over sides. Repeat with 2 more sheets of filo. (Keep filo covered with a damp cloth while not working with it to keep it from drying out.) Add cheese mixture to the pan. Trim filo dough; allow the top edge to extend about 1 1/2 inches above the filling. Fold dough over filling and place trimmed scraps on top. Brush another sheet of filo with butter. Fold in half (butter side in) and lay on top of the filling, shaping to fit pan and folding the edges underneath.

Brush with more butter. Repeat with the remaining 2 sheets of filo. Bake artichoke tart at 400° for 20 minutes. Cover loosely with foil and bake 35 minutes longer.

Makes 10 appetizer servings, served warm or at room temperature.

The following recipes are courtesy of www.InspiredEating.com; originally appearing in the Inspired Eats i-Phone app, available on i-Tunes.

Grilled Baby Artichokes with Blood Oranges and Thyme

Serves 4

- 16 baby artichokes
- 1 medium lemon
- 2 tablespoons olive oil
- 2 tablespoons champagne or white wine vinegar
- Juice and zest of one blood orange (substitute regular orange)
- 1 tablespoon fresh thyme leaves
- 1/8 teaspoon white pepper
- 2 large blood oranges, sliced crosswise 1/2-inch thick
- Whole thyme sprigs for garnish

Fill a medium glass bowl with cold water. Halve lemon and squeeze juice into the water.

Working quickly to prevent browning, cut off and discard stem of artichoke near the base; remove and discard all of the tough outer leaves, leaving only softer, yellowish-green inner leaves, then cut off and discard the top third of the artichoke. Immediately place trimmed artichoke into lemon water to prevent browning.

Repeat with remaining artichokes.

In a large bamboo or stainless steamer, or in a large pot with 1/2 inch water, steam artichokes for 7 minutes, or until bottoms are just tender.

While artichokes are steaming, whisk together olive oil, vinegar, orange juice, orange zest, thyme leaves and white pepper in a small bowl.

Add steamed artichokes and orange slices to the marinade, and gently toss to coat. Let stand at room temperature for 15 to 20 minutes.

While artichokes are marinating, preheat grill. Grill artichokes and oranges for 2 to 3 minutes per side, until artichokes are tender, basting with marinade several times.

Transfer grilled artichokes and oranges to a serving platter, drizzle with additional marinade, garnish with sprigs of fresh thyme, and serve immediately.

Warm Artichokes with Harissa-White Bean Dip

Serves 6 to 8

- 2 medium artichokes
- 2 cups cooked white beans
- 3 tablespoons lemon juice
- 3 garlic cloves, pressed
- 1/4 teaspoon cumin
- 1/3 cup olive oil plus 2 teaspoons
- 1 to 3 teaspoons harissa,* to taste

Cut off artichoke stems, remove bottom leaves, and trim about 1 inch from top of artichokes. Using sharp kitchen shears, trim off top 1/2 inch of each remaining leaf.

Place a steamer rack in a large pot and add just enough water to touch bottom of rack.

Place artichokes on rack and bring water to a boil.

Reduce heat, cover and steam until a leaf near the center of artichoke pulls out easily, 40 to 50 minutes.

(Alternatively, steam artichokes in a pressure cooker for 10 to 15 minutes.)

While artichokes are cooking, combine white beans, lemon juice, garlic, cumin and 1/3 cup of the olive oil in a blender or food processor, and puree until smooth and creamy; add water if needed 1 tablespoon at a time to reach desired consistency. Add harissa, pulse to mix, and taste to adjust for seasonings.

To serve, transfer hummus to one or two dip bowls; drizzle top of hummus with remaining oil. Serve alongside warm artichoke, or remove artichokes leaves and serve alongside hummus for dipping.

Harissa is a spicy Middle-Eastern sauce, available at most large groceries, natural products stores and specialty markets; if you can't find it, substitute Sriracha or a hot sauce of your choice.

Artichoke and Black Olive Tapenade in Radicchio Cups

Makes 6 to 8 appetizer-sized servings

- 3/4 cup pitted Kalamata olives
- 3/4 cup pitted green olives
- 2 tablespoons capers
- 3 garlic cloves, minced
- 1/2 cup chopped raw walnuts
- 8 ounces artichoke hearts, rinsed well
- 1 tablespoon minced rosemary needles
- 2 tablespoons olive oil
- 2 teaspoons lemon juice
- 1/4 teaspoon white pepper
- 1 small head of radicchio
- 1/4 cup chopped parsley
- 1/4 cup toasted pine nuts

Combine olives, capers, garlic, walnuts and artichoke hearts in a food processor. Pulse until ingredients are coarsely chopped.

Add rosemary, olive oil, lemon juice and white pepper, and continue pulsing until all ingredients are finely chopped, but not smooth.

Remove outer leaves from radicchio and discard. Carefully remove all but the smallest inner leaves, leaving leaves intact and whole.

Arrange leaves on a serving platter, concave side up, to form small "cups."

Divide tapenade between radicchio cups and sprinkle with parsley and pine nuts. Serve immediately.

(Tapenade may be made in advance and refrigerated for up to 24 hours before filling cups.)

ARTI-JOKES
Jokes about artichokes

Knock, knock.
Who's there?
Artichokes.
Artichokes, who?
Artichokes when he eats too fast...

Arti was a real loser. Every job and every idea he ever had turned out wrong. He thought to himself, if I went into business for myself, maybe, just maybe I can do well.

He thought and he thought, what could he do. It came to him, he would be a HIT MAN. The next day he put a classified ad in the newspaper reading, "I am Arti, I will be your HIT MAN. Give me a call and I will kill anyone you want rubbed out."

Well that very day Arti receives his first call. The caller asks if it were true that Arti would indeed kill anyone and Arti assured him that was the case. The man told Arti he wanted his wife killed. Arti said, "Fine, but how much will you pay me?"

The man replied, "$1.00."

Arti said, "No way, bullets cost more than that."

The man replied, "Look, take it or leave it. Many people would kill my wife for free, but I don't want to be obligated."

Arti thought it over and figured he could use the practice so he said, "OK, tell me about your wife, how can I find her?"

The man said, "In the produce department at Food-Mart, every day at four o'clock she is there. She wears a yellow outfit and is always complaining about something."

Arti decides that he will go there and choke her. At least he will save himself the cost of bullets. Sure enough, she is in the produce department of Food-Mart complaining about the fruit being either too hard or too soft.

Arti reaches behind her and chokes her. As she fall to the floor, she makes a gasp. The manager of the produce department turns around and sees what has happened and calls out. Arti lunges at the manager and chokes him.

Just as the manager falls to the floor, a lady sees what has happened and screams out. Arti grabs her chokes her and runs out of the supermarket.

He is captured a block away. What does the headline of the newspaper read?

ARTI CHOKES THREE FOR A DOLLAR AT FOOD-MART!

Who is Judy H. Wright aka Auntie Artichoke & What's with the Artichoke?

Judy is a parent educator, family coach and personal historian who has written more than 20 books, hundreds of articles and speaks internationally on family issues, including care giving. Trained as a ready to learn consultant, she works with Head Start organizations and child care resource centers. She also volunteers time writing end-of-life stories for Hospice.

She and Dwain, her husband of 40 years, have six grown children and seven grandchildren. They consider their greatest success in life that their children like themselves and each other. The honorary title of "Auntie" is given in many cultures to the wise women who guide and mentor others in life.

The artichoke also became a teaching lesson when Judy, with her young family, moved into military housing in California to find Artichokes in their yard. Given that it takes two years for the vegetable to flower, the original gardener never got to see the seeds of her labor. Many times, our actions and reactions in life are felt by people we will never meet, but we plant the seeds of kindness anyway.

The symbol of the artichoke has great meaning in her teaching and writing. As she works with families, she sees frequently only the outer edges, which can be prickly, hard to open and sometimes bitter to the taste. They are closed to new ideas or methods. Many families prefer the known over the unknown, even when the old patterns and skills are not serving them well.

But as you expose the artichoke and people to warmth, caring and time, gradually the leaves begin to open and expose the real treasure—the heart.

Judy H. Wright aka Auntie Artichoke
(406) 549-9813

Email: Judy@ArtichokePress.com
www.ArtichokePress.com

"Finding the heart of the story in the journey of life."

"Visiting with Judy is like having a cup of tea with a loving auntie."

Resources for Parents, Teachers and other Caring Adults

http://www.ArtichokePress.com Main website for Judy H Wright, full listing of books, workshops, radio shows, tele-classes. Free report available.

http://www.JudyHWright.com Personal website for Judy H. Wright, including blog and articles. Connect with Judy for empowerment coaching and inspirational speaking engagements.

http://www.BounceBackPerson.com Site for Judy's latest book, *Out Of Balance? Be a Bounce Back Person*. Includes bonus items.

http://www.EmpowermentWithJudy.com Mentoring and MasterMind. Not empowerment for Judy or by Judy, but with Judy. Walking life's journey together.

http://www.KidsChoresandMore.com Site for Judy's book, *Kids, Chores, And More*. Includes bonus items. Free report available.

http://www.TheLeftOutChild.com Site for the importance of friendship, Sign up for our free e-course

http://www.AskAuntieArtichoke.com Blog for parenting and relationships. Please leave comments and questions. You will be glad you did.

http://www.ArticlesbyJudy.com Free articles on relationships/parenting/grief/personal development Free to use in your blog-just keep content and contact info intact.

http://www.IfDeathIsNear.com Blog for those facing the loss of a loved one.

http://www.DeathOfMyPet.com Book and bonus items for someone who has lost a beloved pet.. Excellent stories and resources for pet lovers.

http://www.CyberbullyingHelp.com Main site for bullying and cyberbullying assistance. Free report and connections to other blogs and websites. Leave comments and share your story.

http://www.UseEncouragingWords.com Main site for free e-book on the power of words and communication.

http://www.DisciplineYesPunishNo.com Site for alternatives to punishment. Transform and strengthen your family connections and communications.

http://www.WelcomeAbundance.com Methods of earning passive streams of income.

http://www.EncourageSelfConfidence.com Site for Judy's book, *Using Encouraging Words to Motivate Positive Action* and bonus items about building self-confidence with encouraging words.

http://www.4LifeHappyKids.com/Judy Goal setting and teaching your children the Law of Attraction.

http://www.JudyHWright.com/GiggleBaby Giggle Baby – Find great clothes and creative products for your children

Thank you for joining our community of kind, thoughtful people who want to model and teach kindness, tolerance and respect for all.

Printed in Great Britain
by Amazon